For

For My Son

Compiled by
Barbara Kohn

 PETER PAUPER PRESS, INC.
WHITE PLAINS, NEW YORK

*To my sons, Brian and Steve, who,
along with their sister, Laurie, have
made it possible for me to experience
life's most special pleasure—
motherhood*

Copyright © 1993
Peter Pauper Press, Inc.
202 Mamaroneck Avenue
White Plains, NY 10601
All rights reserved
ISBN 0-88088-750-8
Printed in Singapore
7 6 5 4 3 2 1

FOR MY SON

FOR MY SON

The journey parents and sons take from childhood to adulthood, from dependency to independence, from oneness to individuality, can be both tumultuous and rewarding.

Often the way chosen by our sons is different from our own. If, however, as Ralph Waldo

Emerson said, we "respect the child [and] be not too much his parent," our paths will converge and we will meet in mutual love and understanding.

B. K.

*I*f you can fill the unforgiving
   minute
With sixty seconds' worth of
   distance run,
Yours is the Earth and
   everything that's in it,
And . . . which is more . . .
   you'll be a Man, my Son!
       R UDYARD K IPLING,
               If

When I was a kid my parents
moved around a lot, but I
always found them.

RODNEY DANGERFIELD

Growing up, my father told
me "The reason your feet
point forward is because that's
the direction you must go."
JOHN MACKEY

*B*uild me a son, O Lord, who will be strong enough to know when he is weak, and brave enough to face himself when he is afraid; one who will be proud and unbending in honest defeat, and humble and gentle in victory.

GEN. DOUGLAS MACARTHUR

*O*ur past and our present are in one place. For instance, my grandchild came home from school after learning about the Exodus and he asked his mother if she was with Moses when he left Egypt to come here.

GOLDA MEIR

The worst misfortune that can happen to an ordinary man is to have an extraordinary father.

AUSTIN O'MALLEY

*W*e both like sports, but we cheer for different teams. He's a great swimmer; I like golf. I'm pretty aggressive, but Bradley is a very gentle human being—courteous and sensitive. We really savor our quiet times together, a chance to read, to be introspective. Now over to you, Bradley.

BRYANT GUMBEL

*O*ur dad, Ira, felt at some point in my life that I should give up a lot of that music bull---- and go find a job to support my family. Ira didn't think I was a good enough musician to go on . . .

WILLIE NELSON

I'm only an adopted son. I was born in England and left as soon as I realized I couldn't become king.

BOB HOPE

*H*ow can I explain his [Michael's] success and still be modest? It's in the genes.

KIRK DOUGLAS

I can't spank (my son). If I go
to spank him he says, "You
can't hit me. I'll write a book."

ROBIN WILLIAMS

I could never bring myself to
say what I had planned to say.
"You bum! I have stretch
marks around my knees and
you don't have five minutes to
call your mother."

ERMA BOMBECK

*M*y mother always phones me
and asks, "Is everything all
wrong?"

RICHARD LEWIS

I think he [my father] always thought of me as pretty much of a lightweight. He treated me like he was disappointed in me a lot of the time, and he had every right to be. It has been one of the great agonies of my life that he could never know.

PAUL NEWMAN

Although I am Frank Perdue's son, I wasn't born with confidence. That can only come with victories.

JAMES PERDUE

*Y*ou hear it said that fathers
want their sons to be what they
feel they cannot themselves be,
but I tell you it also works the
other way.

SHERWOOD ANDERSON

O wonderful son, that can so
astonish a mother!

WILLIAM SHAKESPEARE,
Hamlet

*N*o man is responsible for his
father. That is entirely his
mother's affair.

MARGARET TURNBULL

*T*o a young boy, the father is a giant from whose shoulders you can see forever.

PERRY GARFINKEL

*H*e [Willy Loman] wants to live
on through something—and
in his case, his masterpiece is
his son. . . . all of us want that,
and it gets more poignant as
we get more anonymous in
this world.

ARTHUR MILLER

A man who has been the indisputable favorite of his mother keeps for life the feeling of a conqueror, that confidence of success that often induces real success.

SIGMUND FREUD

*I*f you simply convey something as an order, that makes it an issue to rebel against. My son, who is 15, recently asked if he could pierce his ears. When I said he could, he no longer wanted to—at least so far.

DR. ANNE C. PETERSEN

*A*ge 17 is the point in the journey when the parents retire to the observation car; it is the time when you stop being critical of your eldest son and he starts being critical of you.

SALLY AND JAMES RESTON

*M*y father was poor. . . . He thought that with the music there was very little to do, and he thought better to be a carpenter. He was thinking seriously of that for me, but my mother said to him, "This boy has a gift, and it is our duty to follow it." She was a wonderful woman.

PABLO CASALS

*T*hey stood there singing "God Bless America," . . . I looked at these kids—Japanese, Chinese, Jewish, my one black kid—and I started thinking, "Rodney, it's not always so unfair. There are inequities in this world, but not every minute. Not always."

TERRY MCMILLAN

*T*here must always be a
struggle between a father and
son, while one aims at power
and the other at independence.
SAMUEL JOHNSON

*Y*ou've got to do your own
growing, no matter how tall
your grandfather was.

SIR THOMAS OVERBURY

*I*t is a wise child that knows its
own father, and an unusual
one that unreservedly approves
of him.

MARK TWAIN

Again, many possessions, if they do not make a man better, are at least expected to make his children happier; and this pathetic hope is behind many exertions.

GEORGE SANTAYANA

When I started boxing, all I really wanted was someday to buy my mother and father a house and own a nice big car for myself.

MUHAMMAD ALI

I taught them values—always confront the things you fear, try to be the best at whatever you do. That's what my daddy taught me, and those are the things that have to be taught. You don't learn those things by accident.

CASSIUS CLAY, SR.

Any father whose son raises his hand against him is guilty of having produced a son who raised his hand against him.

CHARLES PEGUY

I call it "the experience," [after his son almost died] but really it was a process of healing and growth that enabled me to reorder my priorities in life, to think about my life in a very different way and to relate to people in a very different way,

ALBERT GORE

She (mother) was so deeply imbedded in my consciousness that for the first year of school I seem to have believed that each of my teachers was my mother in disguise.

PHILIP ROTH,
Portnoy's Complaint

*T*he young man knows the rules, but the old man knows the exceptions.

OLIVER WENDELL HOLMES

*T*he child had every toy his
father wanted.

ROBERT E. WHITTEN

Respect the child. Be not too much his parent. Trespass not on his solitude.

RALPH WALDO EMERSON

Sons have always a rebellious
wish to be disillusioned by that
which charmed their fathers.

ALDOUS HUXLEY

Go my sons, burn your books,
Buy yourselves stout shoes.
Get away to the mountains,
   the deserts
And the deepest recesses
   of the earth.
In this way and no other
   will you gain
A true knowledge of things
   and
Of their properties.

SETER SEVERINUS

The father who does not teach
his son his duties is equally
guilty with the son who
neglects them.

CONFUCIUS

I find this same problem exists in all fathers and sons. There is something about the relationship that is pretty difficult to put your finger on. I think fathers realize this and have it on their minds a good deal more than the sons realize.

SHERWOOD ANDERSON

When I was a boy I used to do what my father wanted. Now I have to do what my boy wants. My problem is: When am I going to do what I want?

SAM LEVENSON

*H*ow is it that little children
are so intelligent and men so
stupid? It must be education
that does it.

ALEXANDRE DUMAS,
THE YOUNGER

A king had a son who had gone astray from his father a journey of a hundred days. His friends said to him: "Return to your father." He said: "I cannot." Then his father sent to say: "Return as far as you can, and I will come to you the rest of the way." So God says: "Return to me and I will return to you."

TALMUD

*M*y father was frightened of
his father, I was frightened of
my father, and I am damned
well going to see to it that my
children are frightened of me.

KING GEORGE V

I do not mean to say we are bound to follow implicitly in whatever our fathers did. To do so would be to discard all the lights of current experience—to reject all progress—all improvement.

ABRAHAM LINCOLN

Nearly every man is a firm
believer in heredity until his
son makes a fool of himself.

ANONYMOUS

I have a dream that one day on the red hills of Georgia the sons of former slaves and the sons of former slave owners will be able to sit down together at the table of brotherhood.

MARTIN LUTHER KING, JR.

*I*t is odd how all men develop the notion, as they grow older, that their mothers were wonderful cooks. I have yet to meet a man who will admit that his mother was a kitchen assassin, and nearly poisoned him.

ROBERTSON DAVIES

*T*o be fair to my father, the man spent many years wrestling with a question that no parent has ever been able to answer: *What's wrong with that boy?*

BILL COSBY

*H*ow long does a boy really belong to you? Five, maybe six years. Then for ten years he is a savage, and for the next five years a callow introvert with mental growing pains.

HAL BOYLE

*M*en are what their mothers
made them.

RALPH WALDO EMERSON

I wanted to take my children
to an entertainment, a musical
no less, [Falsettos] that
reinforces the notion that there
are many ways to be masculine,
from selfish to generous, from
brutal to brave, and that it is
up to each boy to make a
choice.

FRANK RICH

We think our fathers fools,
    so wise we grow;
Our wiser sons, no doubt,
    will think us so.

ALEXANDER POPE

A foolish son brings grief to
his father and bitterness to the
one who bore him.

PROVERBS 17:25 (NIV)

*D*o everything right, all the
time, and the child will
prosper. It's as simple as that,
except for fate, luck, heredity,
chance, and the astrological
sign under which the child was
born . . .

ANN BEATTIE,
Picturing Will

*Y*ou young men here may be
in the battle, in the fields or in
the high air. Others will be the
heirs to the victory your elders
or our parents have gained,
and it will be for you to ensure
that what is achieved is not cast
away.

WINSTON CHURCHILL

A wise son brings joy to his father, but a foolish son grief to his mother.

PROVERBS 10:1 (NIV)

*T*he God to whom little boys
say their prayers has a face
very like their mother's.

                JAMES M. BARRIE

*P*eter Pan carried a knife.

LARRY HAGMAN,
when asked how J. R. Ewing
could be the son of
Peter Pan (Mary Martin)

*I*f there were one thing I could say to parents, it would be—*try to enjoy your children. . . .* Throughout my two sons' childhoods . . . I didn't enjoy them nearly as much as I now wish I had.

DR. BENJAMIN SPOCK

*F*rom my mother I learned
that to tolerate cruelty is
cruelty itself. Neglect of any
kind of life is actually a neglect
of God. To love and respect,
and even in a way worship, all
living things is truly to love,
respect, and worship God, the
Creator of all things.

ISAAC BASHEVIS SINGER

Never fret for an only son.
The idea of failure will never
occur to him.

GEORGE BERNARD SHAW

Criticism, like rain, should be
gentle enough to nourish a
man's growth without
destroying his roots.

FRANK A. CLARK

Absalom, my son! Would that
I had died instead of you!

KING DAVID,
after the death of his son